Philip Alfred Emery

Landscapes of History

Philip Alfred Emery

Landscapes of History

ISBN/EAN: 9783337720766

Printed in Europe, USA, Canada, Australia, Japan

Cover: Foto ©ninafisch / pixelio.de

More available books at **www.hansebooks.com**

Landscapes of History.

A Manual Explanatory of Chart,
RELIGION AND SCIENCE:
AND THE
Twelve Axioms of History.

BY P. A. EMERY, M.A.,
Author of "Order of Creation," "Inner Life Night Thoughts;" etc., Founder of "Kansas Deaf-Mute Inst." Principal of Chicago Deaf-Mute School. etc., etc.

THE TWIN RIVERS, A POEM BY J. T. C.

APPENDIX
Containing a brief Biographical Sketch of the Author and a written delineation of his phrenological character.

PUBLISHED BY
MRS. M. A. EMERY,

CHICAGO.
1875.

THE MOST PATIENT OF COMPANIONS,
THE MOST FAITHFUL OF COUNSELLORS,
THE MOST UNTIRING OF HELPERS,
AND THE SINCEREST OF FRIENDS,

MY DEAF-MUTE WIFE,

WHO,

BY HER PATIENT,
ENDURING AND UNWEARIED TOIL IN THE
MAINTENANCE OF OUR FAMILY, DURING THE YEARS THAT I
HAVE BEEN OUT OF PROFESSIONAL EMPLOYMENT, HAS CON-
TRIBUTED SO LARGELY TO THE SUCCESS
OF MY LABORS FOR
THE

GOOD OF OTHERS,

AND THE BENEFIT OF OUR DEAR CHILDREN,
THIS LITTLE VOLUME IS MOST AFFECTIONATELY DEDICATED
BY
THE AUTHOR.

Contents.

---o---

Dedication...	5
Why this Work is Published...................	9
Twelve Axioms of History.....................	13
Amplification of the Axioms.................	17

Explanation of Chart.

Mathematics of History........................	55
Design of Chart..................................	58
The First Golden Age (Fig. 1*)...............	59
The First Silver Age (Fig. 2).................	63
The First Brazen Age (Fig 3).................	67
The First Iron and Clay Age (Fig. 4).......	68
The Second Clay and Iron Age (Fig. 5)....	68
The Second Brazen Age (Fig. 6).............	69
The Second Silver Age (Fig. 7)..............	70
The Second Golden Age (Fig. 8).............	72
The Millennium.................................	74
The End of Time...............................	75
How the Millennium and End of Time is found	76
Why Chart Printed in Colors................	77
Corroborative Testimony.....................	81
Religion and Science compared to Two Rivers—A Poem on Chart..............................	87

---

* Refers to corresponding number on Chart.

Contents of Appendix.

Why this Appendix.................................... 94
BIOGRAPHICAL SKETCH
  Nativity and Parentage........................ 95
  When and How Hearing was Lost................ 96
  Begins Manual a. b. c. at the Ripe Age of 21..... 97
  What Sciences and How they were Studied...... 97
  Motive and Stimulus to so much hard Study...... 99
  Why the Honorary Degree of A. M. was conferred 100
  When and to whom Married.................... 100
  Kansas Life: Famine; "Kansas Deaf-Mute Institute"; "Home Circle," etc.................. 100
  Chart, "Order of Creation,"................... 101
  Chart, "Religion and Science,"................ 102
  As an Educator............................... 103
  Personal Appearances......................... 104
  Is compared to the Founder of the "object system" 105
  His Future predicted.......................... 106
PHRENOLOGICAL CHARACTER
  Organization more for Mental than Physical Labor 109
  "Many Ideas".................................. 110
  Moral and Intellectual Character and Tendency... 112
  Organization for a "good Writer"............. 114
  Inventor...................................... 114
  And a "good Minister," etc.................... 115

Why This Work is Published.

1. A desire to give to others, especially to that large class of persons who have neither the time nor the means of acquiring for themselves, the results of long and patient study and much thought in the form of a Chronology brief, accurate, and always available. To select and extract from a mass of miscellaneous matter the few grains of historical dates, marking the principal events, of scientific, civil and religious history of the world ; and to arrange them in an attractive and useful form, especially adapted to the young, and at the same time not less worthy the attention of the mature of all classes, is the aim of the author.

2. To demonstrate, as perfectly as the limits of the work will permit, that the history of individuals, of nations, and of the

world, both as to science and to religion, is cast in a circular form and is a mathematical problem that can be solved by mathematical rules. Every circle, historical as well as geometrical, is divided by two lines crossing at right angles in the center, and dividing it into four equal parts. These again may be subdivided into as many sections as are necessary, each grand division, half or quarter, being always equal to the other. Take for illustration the history of a man. The time of his life is divided into four principal eras; childhood, youth, manhood, and old age. The full circle of one man's life will vary somewhat from that of another, some scarcely going beyond sixty years, and others attaining to the ripe old age of ninety or one hundred years. But one part will harmonize with the others. Slow development in attaining to maturity will, as a rule, indicate long life, and a rapid development of powers and an unnatural precocity will indicate a rapid decline and a short life. These instances, of course, refer to cases where the circle is fully run, and not cut short by accident or abnormal causes. Hence parents and teachers of science or morals should lead and direct the youthful powers in normal action, and not crowd and *force* them into an unnatural action. The process of cramming and crowding the young of all ages so largely practiced in our public schools, and higher institutions of learning, is highly detrimental to the mental powers, which should be cultivated rather in the use than the mere accumulation of knowledge; and which should not be forced, especially in children, into unnatural tension or into distasteful and repulsive directions. While we believe that early habits of diligence and usefulness are of the utmost importance, the natural bent, inclination and *taste* of the child or youth for any especial trade or profession ought to be *conscientiously* consulted.

3. To show as nearly as may be from the dates in our possession, that as the two halves of anything are equal, one with the other, so the two great periods of the

world's history—the decline of the human race from a golden age of innocence, through a silver, and a copper, to one of iron and clay (Dan. ii, 31–33) and the return—must correspond one with the other as to their principal dates, events, and order of progressions. It will be seen by a reference to our manual that we have demonstrated that the full inauguration of the Millennial era is yet in the somewhat distant future, and will be reached only through the orderly progress of the race in natural and spiritual regeneration.

4. We ask for our little work a patient and careful examination, a candid and kindly criticism, and a friendly and fraternal acceptance of its truths and forbearance with its errors. We are all of one family, all enduring the same imperfections and evils, all aspiring to the same great end, happiness and peace, and it becomes us all to contribute our utmost to the great work of the world's redemption and final glory.

Chicago, Ill., 1875. P. A. E.

AXIOMS OF HISTORY.

Twelve Axioms of History.

1. History is based upon the rotations of humanity on the dial of time. Fig. 1-8*; P. 17†.

2. Sacred History is the record, written or unwritten, of the evolution of internal human science. P. 19†

3. Profane History is the record, written or unwritten, of the evolution of external human science. P. 23†

4. Retrogression is an internal downward, and progression an internal upward movement of man, which is ultimated on the external plane, and noted on the dial of time. P. 27†

---

* Refers to figures on Chart—"Religion and Science."
† Refers to pp. in manual to Chart   do   do

5. Man's internal state is the cause of his external retrogression or progression; hence, his outward corresponds to his inward state. P. 30†

6. Former states with the race, as with individuals, never return. Human cycles are spirals, not planes. P. 32†

7. "History repeats itself"—not identically; but each cycle rises, step by step, on the ladder of time—first internally, and then externally. P. 34†

8. The history of religion keeps pace with that of science; and man's internal nature is potent in making his external history.*— P. 36†

9. Religion is the aspiration of the human for the Divine, and is an impulse implanted in all men. P. 38†

10. Idolatry—abnormal religion—is the inverted use of man's religious nature; by heathen in idol worship, by Christendom in the love of rule, of pleasure, of honor, and of wealth—the love of self and the world.— P. 40†

---

* Sickness, wars, pestilence, etc., are caused by man's abnormal spiritual state. P. 65.

11. Arcana Cœlestia and Natura are correlated as soul and body, religion the soul, science the body—microcosm and macrocosm. P. 46†

12. When the spiritual and the natural arcana are correctly understood, and their laws fully obeyed, then, not before, will humanity enter the millennial state or second Golden Age; then will be completed the first round on the human dial of time. P. 51†

AMPLIFICATIONS
OF
AXIOMS OF HISTORY.

AN AMPLIFICATION

OF THE

Twelve Axioms of History;

OR THE

Fall and Rise of Religion and Science.

AXIOM I.

History is based upon the rotations of humanity on the dial of time. Fig. 1—8.*

1. Motion, in its primary elements, is of two forms; the circular and the linear. The variations of these and their combinations give us all the varieties known, in mechanics and nature. The linear, under varied impulses becomes zig-zag, irregular and angular. The circular, in like manner, becomes undulatory, rolling and spiral.

The circular has respect to beauty, harmony and good; the linear, to brilliancy, magnificence and truth. The spiral, to the progressions of goodness by truth to development and use.

---

* Refers to figures on Chart—" Religion and Science."

2. The moral evolutions of man have reference to his quality as to good ; the scientific, as to truth   In the former, man's course is in a circle or ellipse ; while in the latter, it is angular and forward from point to point.* It is this variety of condition and state with man that is the foundation of all history. The union of good and truth in the Creator, and their united communication to all creation cause and necessitate progression and development in all created things as a primary law of their existence. Did good exist alone without truth, all things would move in a fixed, unvarying circle ; and did truth exist alone without good, all things would fly off in a tangent, without an end or use. The perfect combination of these principles in creation gives development, progression and use.

3. History results from the combined orbital and forward movements of the race, morally and scientifically, socially and politically,

---

* See Paths of Religion and Science on Chart. Religion is represented by the winding *red* path; and Science by the zig-zag *blue* path.

internally and externally. It is germinated within, and ultimated without in the deeds of men and nations. The rise, development, consummation and decay of nations and peoples, has been repeated over and over again; and will continue so to be repeated till the restoration of all things and the redemption of the race.

AXIOM II.

Sacred History is the record, written or unwritten, of the evolution of internal human science.

1. Sacred history is the record of the fluctuations of the church. The church consists in the principles of spiritual science and its indwelling life, evolved and developed through various dispensation, especially as revealed in the sacred Word of God. The Word from first to last is a repository of spiritual science as applicable to man, vailed in an allegorical account of creation and the early history of the race, and a fragmentary history of a single people. The history of creation as given in the first chapters of Genesis, is true in sub-

stance and in fact, but is allegorical as to time and the method of creative procedure. Facts of science, especially those of geology, prove the process to have extended over vast ages instead of six ordinary days of time. The primary significance of the account lies in its correspondence with the internal moral recreation of man from a state of chaos, darkness and moral death into which he had degenerated since the inversion of order in his internal nature.

2. The waters upon which the Spirit of God moved were the falsities of a disorderly science, generated in the mind by its inverted action in making the sensual and external the supreme, and by reasoning from natural scientifics as causes to spiritual results as effects. The light which shone upon the darkness, was the light of pure spiritual truth or science, let into the mind—revealing its darkness, vacuity and moral chaos. The light is pronounced good, orderly—genuine truth—and there was then a distinction made between the darkness of false science in the

mind, and the inbeaming truth of genuine science let in from the superior degree above. And the light was called day, and the darkness night,—and the evening (falsity) and the morning (truth) were the first day (or state with man).

That this is the primary significance of this account may be further seen by the fact that the two great lights and all the lesser lights—sun, moon and stars—were not created until the fourth day; whereas in the actual course of creation they undoubtedly preceded the first beginnings of the earth by long ages. It is clearly established that the earth proceeded from the sun as its source, and that the stars are evidently much more ancient than the sun itself. The whole account is, without doubt, written from the point of man's regeneration, and is a correspondential account of the progress of good and truth in the human soul and mind. Thus we have the productions of the vegetable kingdom prior to the existence of the sun, which is, in truth, the sole vivifying influence of nature.

With this correspondential interpretation all becomes clear, harmonious and rational. Life in the soul is generated by the over-brooding Spirit, after the admission of light—truth—and the re-ordering of the chaotic elements, and their separation and arrangement into some order, while yet the principle of Love (the sun), and wisdom (the moon), and the knowledges of faith (the stars) were inoperative with man in a degree sufficient to enable him to produce any acts from genuine good; signified by living creature that moveth and winged fowl that fly, and creeping things and cattle and beast of the earth: things that have some life. Man can produce nothing which is good in itself so long as he works from himself, for the selfhood is evil, and all things that flow from it are of a like quality. But when Love to the Lord becomes the dominant principle and source of action, and charity the prevailing social condition, he then for the first time begins to live, and his works have life, and are good.

AXIOM III.

Profane History is the record, written or unwritten, of the evolution of external human science. F. 1—8.*

1. The science of humanity embraces all the questions of individual obligations, social problems and political rights, with all questions of industry—labor, commerce, the arts and sciences, literature and religion—in short, all that concerns a people and conduces to their progress and well being. History is the record of the experience of a people in these various interests; the record of the experiments made and the results obtained, the conclusions drawn and the courses adopted, the laws enacted and the effects of all these on the welfare of the people.

2. Profane history is the record of all the experiences, vicissitudes, fluctuations and catastrophes of individuals, nations, and peoples that have passed across the stage of life and left their impress upon the human race—religions and their influences alone excepted.

---

* Refers to figures on Chart—"Religion and Science."

It is the province of history to faithfully record the entire experience of the age and people of which it treats; as well the mistakes, the defeats, the disasters, as the triumphs, the victories, the successes; as well the faults, the crimes as the virtues; that the images of its reflections be not distorted, the lessons of its teaching be not lost, and the great end for which it was instituted be accomplished.

3. The human race, like each individual of it, has its infancy, its childhood, its youth and its manhood; and these conditions are attained by the development of germinal possibilities which are infolded in the embryo from its first germinal existence; awaiting only the age and the necessary conditions for development into positive, active and potential being. It is the struggling forth of these germinating powers through the superincumbent mass of gross perversions and abnormal conditions that have fallen upon the race through the inversions of individual, social and political order; that causes the

great upheavings of human society, and the downfall and extinction of nations, which form so large a part of human history and cause one to wonder at the terrible ruin attending the birth of a world. Had our race escaped the fearful inversions of Divine Order that have come upon it, the task of History as a chronicler of human experience had been one of unmixed delight and the record but an exultant song of continual triumph.

4. We may suppose the normal development of a race to be without violent and sudden changes, without great social or political or industrial upheavals, without catastrophe; we may suppose it to be harmonious and orderly like the growth of a tree, or the progressions of the seasons, through bud and blossom and ripened fruit to a finished use and the glorious consummation of a divinely ordered destiny. We may suppose that Divine Order is like the Divine Being Himself, Perfect Harmony, and we must look to some opposing force, some antagonistic power in nature and man for a solution of the other-

wise insoluble problem of disorder in the world of nature and humanity. That power we find, not in the inevitable law of evolution from a *pointless* beginning without creation, through myriads of *pointless* additions of faculties, powers and attributes, also without creation, up to the consummation of development where evolution ceases—not in the inherent and necessary viciousness of imperfection, necessitating the outgrowth of order from disorder, of harmony from discord, of peace from turbulence, combat and the universal clash and crash of elements;—that power we find not in the hypothesis that order and disorder, good and evil, truth and falsity are only relative conditions of the same things, but in the fact that with man on our earth the normal condition, the original order has become inverted, giving birth to a state of positive, direct and potential antagonism to order, and hence presenting the phenomena of war, conflict and catastrophe in the world.

AXIOM IV.

Retrogression is an internal downward, and progression an internal upward movement of man, which is ultimated on the external plane, and noted on the dial of time.

1. Progression is the first law of all created existences; it is the necessary result of their finite nature. The Infinite Self-existent, alone, is in unprogressive perfection. Creatures receptive of life, and receiving their existence from some source foreign to themselves *and at a germinal point*, must of necessity continue to advance so long as the reception continues, because continued reception necessitates continued increase.

2. Creation is necessarily finite. The Infinite cannot create the Infinite; for that would be self-creation. All creation, formation or production is on a plane *discretely below* the creator or producer. God cannot create anything having life in itself; man cannot make anything receptive of life; and a man-made machine cannot be produced, that, undirected by man, can produce anything. These are self-evident truths.

3. Creation proceeds forth in germs, from the Infinite, to the ultimate or lowest condition of the finite, where it commences its manifestation and individualization, and its return and endless approach toward its Infinite yet ever unattainable source. With creation in its normal condition, retrogression is impossible. The Creator has placed the ultimate at the lowest normal limit of being. Normal progress begins at that point, and must of necessity be forward and upward. Evil alone is abnormal, and is the inversion of all things of order. Retrogression is the inverted movement away from the Creator and toward a point of ultimate extinction of existence. Persistent retrogression is certain destruction, because progress cannot cease nor a state of fixed immovability ensue. Consequently the fixed law of progressive evil or inverted action is self-destruction.

4. The retrogression of the race was from an inversion of order, by which the external and lower usurped rule over the internal and higher faculties of man, thus reversing the

order of creation. Man thus placed external science on the throne and imprisoned internal truth;* till at length the prisoner was forgotten, and he, man, lost all knowledge of spiritual things and became utterly sensual in all the consciousness of his being. The imprisoned spiritual nature remained in a germinal condition awaiting the time of its release, like hidden seeds in the swathings of a mummy,—dormant for ages; yet not destroyed; until at length, the revealment of true science again opened the prison doors and the captive was liberated to become the evangel of life, and a return was inaugurated and progression once more became the law of evolution.† True science is now being reinstated in its rightful position as the internal regulator of the rational man, and the guide to scientific explorations in the kingdom of nature.

---

* See Chart, "Religion and Science," where the Word is being submerged in the waters of the flood near the close of the first age.

† Refers to the establishment of the new spiritual church, represented at the bottom of dial on the Chart by the cross.

AXIOM V.

Man's internal state is the cause of his external retrogression or progression; hence, his outward corresponds to his inward state.

1. Creation is from a central point outward to the circumference. Life flows into man, not from the outward to the inward, but from within outward; because the inmost of the soul is the point of entrance where the divine influence commences, and is beyond the consciousness and in inner darkness. The interior and inmost faculties are in order, the external and its internal are alone subject to disorder and inversion, consequently to retrogression. As is this internal so is its external, for life proceeds from the inmost through the internal to the external. As is the form of the internal vessels receiving life, so will be the form of the life externally exhibited and the quality of its fruits produced. The life flowing in through a grafted tree is the same in both the tree and the grafted branch, but the fruits are various. It is not the ori-

ginal influx that determines the quality of the fruit, but the form of the ultimate organs into which it is received.

2. Life is a unit in all nature, but its manifestations are innumerable—depending on reception. There is natural life, spiritual life, celestial life, all from the Divine life of the Creator. The natural comes through the spiritual, the spiritual through the celestial, the celestial from the Divine in a continual series, a chain of cause and effect.— The external is the ultimate or last link in the chain, and derives its quality from its *immediate* internal, not from the more remote interior or inmost.

3. Man, in his external life, expresses his internal nature. He outlives his inward self. Given the internal condition of a people, the moral quality, the ruling principle, and a prediction of their ultimate history will be approximately, almost positively, correct.— A low, brutal, savage people will have a bloody record, marked deeds of violence and

cruelty totally inhuman. A simple, childlike and gentle people, however ignorant and low in the scale of intellect, will have a mild and peaceful history unmarked by deeds of violence and blood. A pastoral people will have no brilliant military records, nor a mercantile people any splendid triumph in science. Men's achievements lie on the line of their mental and moral endowments and resulting habits of life.

AXIOM VI.

Former states with the race, as with individuals, never return. Human cycles are spirals, not planes.

1. All things revolve in endless circles, and that not on a fixed plane but in continually rising spirals. The experience of to-day is not repeated on the morrow. The point of return is higher or lower than the point of departure, as progression or retrogression is the active condition of the being. Emotions once experienced never return with the same intensity as at first. A pleasure

once tasted loses somewhat of its flavor, and requires an increase of seasoning to render it palatable. A truth reviewed is less brilliant than at its first conception. An exposure to a vivid light leaves the vision less sensitive to a milder radiance.

2. The cycles of time are like the orbits of the sidereal universe—interinvolved the smaller in the greater—from the pulse-beat of an insect to the age of a world. "The end is in the beginning" and infolded in the germ lies all the possibilities of the perfect creature. Moments, hours, days, years and ages are all inorbited, one within another, going forward in the great cycle of a regenerating world. God's moments are centuries, His days as thousands of years, His years as the ages of worlds and universes.

AXIOM VII.

"History repeats itself"—not identically; but each cycle rises, step by step, on the ladder of time—first internally, and then externally.

1. Great historical epochs are similar in general character, but varied with the changing conditions of the race. A dissimilar similarity is characteristic of events as it is of all things of creation. Similarly there are prominent features that mark their individuality. The world does not stamp its heroes with the same die nor cast its great events in the same mold. Ages and conditions bring their events, and events produce their heroes, and heroes write their name in deeds that in turn remold the ages and the conditions.

2. There have been many traitors, but one Judas Iscariot. There have been many tyrants, but one Nero. There have been many unjust judges, but one Jeffries. Many artists have arisen, but Angelo is unequaled in the grandeur and variety of his works. Many great poets have sung, but Milton is peerless

in the sublime sweetness of his song. Many dramatic masters have written, but no second Shakespeare is possible till a *greater* than he shall arise. There have been lawgivers in all ages, but Moses has had no compeer in the history of the race. Many prophets have come to us to warn the people, but none other in the sublime strains of Isaiah.

Every age brings its necessities, and its great characters to meet those necessities.

"Nothing new beneath the sun,
Is a truth but half-expressed;
Nature makes a spiral run,
Moving when she seems at rest;
Moving in a sweep of progress
On to destiny sublime,
Bearing all her eras with her
Down the trackless fields of time.

Naught returns to meet its starting,
Times come back, but not the same—
From a moving point departing
Circles are such but in name.
History *rewrites* her pages,
Not repeats them, o'er and o'er,—
Though while floating down the ages
Past an ever-changing shore,
Every billow that upbears us
Seems like that which rolled before."

AXIOM VIII.

The history of religion keeps pace with that of science; and man's internal nature is potent in making his external history. F. 1—8.*

1. It is said that man is a religious being, and his record in all times gives evidence of the truth of the proverb. Some kind of religion has existed in all ages, and it enters largely into the history of all nations, tribes and people. Its history runs parallel with that of the domestic, industrial, civil and scientific attainments of the people. It is one of the constituents of national life. A people without a religion would be as anomalous as a people without a science adapted to their intellectual condition. Though not dependent the one upon the other for their existence, religion and science are necessarily associated together, having their origin in the dual nature of the human spirit. The one is the product of the will, the moral and affectional nature; the other of the understanding, the rational and intellectual nature.

---

* Refers to figures on Chart—"Religion and Science."

The one is a sentiment or the result of a sentiment, the other an idea or the result of thought. The one springs from the spontaneous cravings of the moral nature; the other is the result of observation, comparison, analysis, thought—a variety of intellectual activities and mental operations.

2. Religion, which is a sentiment, should be carefully distinguished from Theology, which is a science. Science and Theology may easily be variant, or antagonistic, but science and religion never. It is easy to see how our theories of religion, or our religious ideas, may conflict with our theories of science, but not our religious instincts, which are not ideas but sentiments,—unless, indeed, our supposed science goes so far as to destroy the object of our religious aspirations. Science cannot destroy religion nor religion subvert science. The great error of many scientists and of a host of petty aspirants to scientific honors is in charging upon *religion* the faults, the errors, the falsities, and the

crimes of false and corrupt religious *theories* and of wicked ecclesiastical bodies and corrupt ecclesiastical systems.

3. As man is in his moral and intellectual nature, so will be the records of his life. Acts, words, and thoughts go forth from him an utterance of himself; they are the third attribute of the finite trinity of his being.—They are the human proceeding and operative spirit; they form the ultimate sphere and influence of his life.

AXIOM IX.

Religion is the aspiration of the human for the Divine, and is an impulse implanted in all men.

1. Religion as an instinct, as an involuntary motion of the moral nature, is innate in the race. It is a characteristic of humanity necessarily sequent upon his derivation from the Divine Creator. Although greatly perverted it still is the flavor of the fruit, the fragrance of the flower, the magnetic exhalation of the mineral, the indestructible aroma of the moral nature. It is the putting

forth of the moral *antennæ*, the groping in darkness for a vaguely felt presence, the rebound of the unformed, nebulous, chaotic spiritual consciousness of man toward the Being who sent it forth into the soul.

2. Men, even under the deepest degradation, naturally turn toward some unseen superior being, who holds in his hands the threads of destiny,* and who can lead them to good or ill according to his whim, or passion or supreme pleasure. This instinctive sense of dependence, this innate consciousness of moral accountability is the distinguishing feature that characterizes the human discreted from the animal nature. The possibility of knowing right from wrong, not from their consequences, but from their intrinsic natures, and their effects on others, on society and the world, is the superior degree in which manhood is founded. And this tacit acknowledgment of accountability to a superior being, this implanted *possibility* of knowing God, this moral sense, however

---

* See centre illustration on Chart.

perverted, yet that is not quite destroyed even in the lower races, renders man capable of the highest attainments in human perfection.

AXIOM X.

Idolatry—abnormal religion—is the inverted use of man's religious nature; by heathen in idol worship, by Christendom in the love of rule, of pleasure, of honor, and of wealth—the love of self and the world.

1. This religious aspiration, when it becomes inverted and abnormal, is manifested in the various forms of idolatry, whether that of the image worshipers of all heathen nations, the crocodile worshipers of India, the Fire worshipers of Persia, the Sun worshiper of Mexico or the *self* worshipers of Christendom—in all it is the inversion of the pure and orderly religious sentiment. Its orderly operation is to go forth toward the Creator, lifting itself upward and inward to its divine Source; but in its disorderly action, like that of every other faculty of inverted human nature, it goes downward and

outward to the lowest things of nature. We do not find image worshipers bowing to the beautiful, the pure, the highest ideal of human excellence, but to the monstrous, hideous, disgusting and beastly forms— half beast and half demon—the most degraded conceptions of passion and brutality possible to the perverted imagination of degraded beings—real effigies, perhaps, of the demons that surround them in the subtler parts of nature.

2. This principle of idolatry rises with the rise of nations in science and art, and in civil and social progress. But it is still the same perversion of the true religious sentiment that actuates the image-worshiper, the fire-worshiper or the self-worshiper. It is as prevalent in Christendom as in heathen lands, and is as blindly and abjectly followed by the cultured, the refined in Europe and America as it is by the ignorant devotee that immolates herself on the funeral pyre of India.

AXIOM XI.

Arcana Cœlestia and Natura are correlated as soul and body, religion the soul, science the body—microcosm and macrocosm.

1. There are two grand divisions of creation, discreted from each other in substance, but intimately connected by correspondence in form; that is to say, for every natural and material form and creature, there is a spiritual form and creature exactly similar thereto, existing within it, form in form, organ in organ, atom in atom—from the greatest to the least; from a sun to a mustard seed, from man to the least infinitesimal living organism of microscopic revelation. Indeed, the spiritual is the real substance, the real creature; and the material, the manifestation of it. Material substance is in itself dead, inert, and wholly passive; receiving and retaining whatsoever impression is stamped upon it, until it is removed by another, molding it to a new form and condition. Spiritual substance is a discrete degree nearer the Divine Essence, and is essentially active, not

in itself, but from the Divine Life which flows immediately into it, and stands to matter and material life and forms, as cause to effect. Hence the Divine energy and activity living in the spiritual, is, through it, by correspondence of form to form, communicated to the material, causing it to live and to assume forms of life correspondent with the Divine Idea.

2. All creation exists germinally in the Divine Wisdom of the Lord. Those creation germs contain within themselves the embryonic forms of the perfect creature in its own class or species—neither more nor less; and those germinal forms are as infinitely various as are the distinct species of creatures existing in creation. Reproduction is not an inherent or implanted faculty of created things, but it is caused by the deposits of the germ in the reproduction vessels of the creature—whether it be plant, or animal, or man—where external form is assumed through the agency of those organs and not from any creative power within them. All

created things are a system of organs or vessels and contain nothing, in themselves, of life or power,—contain, in themselves, no germs or seeds, but receive and nourish and develop and give birth to them. Their reproductive functions are purely as molds to give form, and as nurseries to impart substance to the germ, and they have no reproductive power whatsoever. All reproduction is from the Lord alone, and a distinct step or advance from a lower to a higher grade in being is not by an added faculty to an existing germ, but by a new germ containing the new faculty. Every new type in creation is from a new germ containing all the features, faculties and *possibilities* of the new type. Creation is not by development of new faculties and attributes from old forms, but by new forms *superimposed* upon lower supporting ones. Man is not derived from the ape, nor the ape from the tadpole; but man took his position at the head of creation, when the conditions were in readiness and the plane prepared for him, in a new organization for the first time formed, with all the attribute and possibilities of manhood complete in their germinal existence. Hence evolution, as understood by scientists of this day, is purely an appearance, and wants the first undeniable *fact* on which to rest its claims for acceptance as the true doctrine of creation.

3. The necessity of the evolution hypothesis to account for creation, disappears with the acknowledgment of the Lord as the creator through germinal points *formed* in His own being and sent forth to receive their various clothing upon in the celestial, spiritual and ultimate kingdoms, and through them down to the natural basis in the natural world. These germs are not things in themselves, but are systems of organs receptive of life, strictly corresponding with their final external forms; and they constitute the inmost degree of being, where the life from the Lord, the Creator, first enters the spiritual organism. When the development is free and not checked or diverted by any foreign force, the full capacity of the original germ

will be perfected in the resulting external form—no power remaining dormant for ages, waiting conditions of development. The Creator is not confined to one germ for all grades of creation, bringing out power by power through the slow unfoldings of ages between each advance in the evolution of the creature, nor to the necessity of allowing myriads of myriads of the slumbering germs of angels to perish in the forms of apes and tadpoles and the thousand links of being below and above them to man!

4. When the great central truth is recognized, that God is the Creator of the universe, not in generals but in particulars, not by masses but by atoms, and not by races but by individuals; and when the fact is also recognized that He is the *only* creator, and that He cannot *possibly* endow any creature with that divine faculty in any degree, nor through the operation of any law, the Arcanas of spirit and nature will become luminous, and naturalists will cease searching for the principle of life and reproduction in the

creature, and will recognize all the intermediate links of being between the first and the last, not as the undeveloped portions of one being, but as the mediums by which the divine descends from the highest to the lowest and returns from the lowest to the highest in creation.

AXIOM XII.

When the spiritual and the natural arcana are correctly understood, and their laws fully obeyed, then, not before, will humanity enter the millennial state, or second Golden Age; then will be completed the first round on the human dial of time.

1. A millennial age has been the day-star, the silver gleam of morning upon the mountain tops, the prophecy of a full-orbed golden day to the world, since the Apocalyptic vision cast its mystic light athwart the darkness of a sensual and benighted age. Men have looked for its coming in the near future all along down the centuries, since the first prophetic annunciation went forth from Patmos that the "tabernacle of God is with men, and He will dwell with them, and they shall

be His people, and God himself shall be with them their God"! They are still looking for the Lord to appear in the clouds of heaven, coming in external physical form to assume the throne of empire over the whole earth and to reign in great glory a thousand years. So confident are they that His coming will be in a visible, objective, material human shape; so sure are they that He will personally and literally walk the earth again as He did over 1800 years ago, that they venture to predict the year and even the day of His appearing; and still, after repeated failures, they again set themselves to reconstruct their calculations and frame their predictions anew, confident that another failure is impossible! This amazing confidence is inconceivable, except on the hypothesis that it is based on some real spiritual fact which, though they fail to perceive it, presses upon the inner consciousness with irresistible power. There is a spirit of truth within this external error that gives it an obscure vitality, that causes the foreshadowings of great events to fall on the soul, like a felt but unseen presence, moving the inner instincts to a remote recognition of its existence.

2. Men fail to see the significance of present events. Their very nearness prevents their comprehension as a whole, distracting the attention to various minor details, of little importance in themselves though necessary to the correct estimate of the grand totality. A farther remove narrows the angle so that it falls fully into the range of vision. We largely judge the present and future by the records of the past. We allow for no progress in our computations of events to come. We assume that any great event that has once transpired must, if it be repeated, occur in the same identical form as before. We omit to note our driftings, and mark our soundings on the edge of our craft, expecting to find them again by casting the line where those markings occur. Thus we look for the second coming of the Lord to be but a glorified repetition of His first advent. We expect Him to walk the earth in outward

visible form, not as a man of sorrows but as King triumphant; not dwelling in the hearts of a regenerated humanity, but inhabiting the sanctuary of the holy city, New Jerusalem, which shall literally dsecend from God out of heaven. Thus we are married to the past, and fail to see the coming Bridegroom.

3. That the dawn of the Millennial day will be characterized by certain great phenomenal catastrophes in the natural world as well as irruptions and upheavals in society and the civil and political world, it is but reasonable to conclude from the fact that all events occurring in the spiritual kingdom, must necessarily produce their corresponding effects outworked in the natural kingdom of creation, and the external affairs of men. But that these events will be of the nature of a literal and bodily appearing of the Lord on earth, and of the physical resurrection and glorification of the Saints, marking the day and hour sharply and definitely, is not in accordance with the revelations of the Spiritual Arcana. The Lord's coming is first

in a new and fuller revelation of spiritual truth, and afterward in a special descent of His Spirit into the purified hearts and affections and thence into the lives of all earnest and faithful regenerating men and women. This is a truth that is now beginning to force itself upon the convictions of most earnest and intelligent religious thinkers.

4. The cravings of the inner nature for a fuller and better life are beginning to make themselves felt; the importunate longings of an unsatisfied heart are prompting many to cry out, "Who will show us any good?" The descent of the heavenly influx is more and more into the things of life. The enlightenment of the intellect fails to satisfy the longings of the heart. The glitter, the resplendence, the glory of spiritual truth is not celestial meat to the famished soul. From the cold, clear brilliancy of a winter's day we turn to the golden fervor of a summer morning. Life, warm, throbbing, communicative life, not cold, statuesque beauty, is the demand of the incoming era. Earth is

awakening from the torpor of her long winter, to the vernal activities of her tropical age.

5. The Coming of the Lord will not be by a revelation of the natural form to the objective and sensuous vision, but by a special revealment of His Divine Human Person to the inner, subjective sight of his humble, obedient, regenerate children. It will be a re-incarnation of the Lord, not in one human person, but into the souls and bodies and fullness of the lives of the whole human race that will receive Him. This re-incarnation will take place only through the personal regeneration of the individual, the personal purifying of each heart, and the subjugation of each will to the full control of His Spirit. He will walk the earth, not outwardly to the recognition of the world, but in the hearts and lives, in the opened and joyous consciousness of his immediate presence in the inmost degree, the holy of holies, of the purified souls of His servants. His children shall walk with Him in white, but it must be the whiteness of perfect innocence. "The pure

in heart shall see God." As each soul attains to the millennial state of perfect regeneration even in this life, the Lord will dwell with him, and he will become a burning, glowing point in the darkness of the age, whence the light and heat of the new life will radiate; and as these points increase so will increase the return of "the days of old and the former times." It is therefore imperative with every one, to strive to enter into the beginnings and to persevere to the fullness of Millennial state, and to no longer look for some great and sudden descent of irresistible power ; nor, on the other hand, to put off the coming of the great and terrible day of the Lord to the far future, looking for but the slow, almost imperceptible, increase of the kingdom of truth. The march of events is accelerated daily. The inconceivable activity and intensity of the spiritual life is descending very closely to the natural world. Life-times are now crowded into a few years, years are compressed into months, and months of activity fill but a few hours' time. When the spiritual and natural arcana are correctly understood, and their laws fully obeyed, then, and not till then, will the human race enter the millennial state, and then will be ushered in the inconceivable glories and beatitudes of the Second Golden Age.

EXPLANATION OF CHART.

Explanation of Chart.

---o---

Mathematics of History.

1. The arrangement of this Chart is based upon mathematical principles, on the same principles that underlie and are the foundation of the construction and regulation of the Universe. Its framework consists of lines and angles; its covering and adornments consist of circles and undulations. Every circle contains the perpendicular and horizontal lines; the perpendicular corresponds to good, and the horizontal to truth. These divide the circle into four equal parts, which correspond to the four seasons of the year and the four points of the compass. On the perpendicular the higher corresponds to greater good, the lower to lesser good; on the horizontal the right or east corresponds

to more light, and the left or west to less light.

2. Each subdivision of the circle is marked on both sides by corresponding dates, going backward and forward from A. D. at the bottom. The upper portion is necessarily in obscurity as to dates, owing to their remote antiquity, on the one hand, and the unrevealed future, on the other. As the declension of the race was from the innocence of infancy and comparative ignorance through the obliteration of perception and love in the west (left) down to the extreme limit of degradation at the bottom, the return from thence would naturally correspond in character and general conditions to the departure. The events would correspond as to character and time throughout the whole circle until the return was complete. We claim this to be the true state of the case, and, taking our best chronology as to dates, we have, we think, fully demonstrated this position. The coincidences are certainly remarkable.

3. The science of mathematics is the only

exact science, and it is the foundation, the frame-work, the skeleton of all science. It is this science that gives firmness and fixity to all others. Spiritual mathematics teaches that the end is in the beginning and that both exist in the Origin; that a circumference necessitates a centre, and that the centre is the cause of the circumference; that the Creator (centre) is necessarily superior to the combined creation; that a general cannot subsist without all of its particulars; that a return necessitates the re-traversing the ground or pathway of the departure and that in the exact inverse order; and that, when the extreme point of departure is reached and a new power intervenes to inaugurate a return, that power will always remain predominant or superior to all opposition,—in other words, when one power is conquered in the utmost exertion of its might by a greater, that conquering power must ever remain superior and triumphant.

4. On these self-evident principles this chart is constructed, and we now proceed to its explanation.

Design of the Chart.

1. This Chart is designed to illustrate the progress of human history—or, more exactly speaking, to show the real pathway, moral and social, religious and scientific, traveled by the human race since its first departure from order to the present time; showing it to have been in the form of a great moral circle or elliptic, passing from its first and orderly condition to the extreme of moral distance, where it became submerged, as to its spiritual condition, in the profound darkness of the " valley of the shadow of death," and from whence it emerged into a new spiritual light at the coming of the Lord. Since then it is, with various vicissitudes, gradually returning toward its former state. During the declension of the race in spiritual life, and the almost total obliteration of internal knowledge, the light of science very slowly and gradually increased and the external scientifics of religion were slowly developed.— Thus, as the race became sensual and corporeal, the intellectual nature only struggled

upward into something of a twilight illumination, its feeble rays giving birth to many spectral images, which were magnified into gigantic proportions, but which, seen in the more perfect light of the advancing dawn, dissolved into the retiring shadows of a superstitious age. Thus the Astrology of the earlier times was but a shadow of the real science of Astronomy and its yet unfolding mysteries of solar and planetary influences, and the alchemy of the early experimentalists was but the mystic vapors that then filled the now-illuminated laboratory of the Chemist. As the great orb of science wheels along the southern sky, those mystic shadows swing backward behind the upstanding facts and are lost in the obscurity of a never-recurring past!

The First Golden Age.

1. In the left hand half of the upper portion of the circle (See Chart, Fig. 1, and also in Daniel ii. 32.) is seen the illuminated representation of the golden age of the

world; that early and better age when the race was in the innocence and purity of a celestial infancy, when the light of the Divine Presence filled the earth with a mild and golden splendor, when harmony reigned through the busy day, and peace crowned the luminous night with a starry glory. Then heaven rested upon the pure unstained earth and angels were frequent visitants to the obedient children of men. (See Genesis i. 26–30.) Then charity had perfect rule and man loved his neighbor as himself. The atmosphere of heaven infilled the air of earth, and men respired in unison with the angels of God. Open intercourse was maintained with the "forefather land," and men were instructed by the immediate revelations of truth from the "most excellent Glory." The great dome of the spiritual mind was illuminated by the Sun of heaven, whose beatific beams descended and lit up the natural understanding with an open perception of truth. Then men were content to be led by the Lord alone, and counted themselves as of little worth aside from the Divine Life within them. To them the Lord was All in All, and their human consociates were dearer than self, and to live and do for others was the height of human happiness. With them the speech was largely tacit, the ideas of the mind finding ready expression in the play of the features. Hypocrisy and deceit were impossible, so luminous was the face with ideas and emotions of the soul.

2. But this condition did not last. The seeds of disorder had once been sown in the earth. Some gigantic evil influence had penetrated the paradise of man ; some anarchical power had gained a footing in the outermost regions of nature, through which the lower faculties of man were exposed to an unnatural and undue stimulus that caused an exaggerated development of the sensuous nature, amounting, at length, to a disorderly condition immediately productive of the beginnings of evil. Men were led gradually and imperceptibly into an undue regard for the things of sense, and the inferior aspired to a

predominance over the superior degrees in the human organism. This degenerate, abnormal, and inversive action continued until at length the whole man became inverted, not only in the order of his being, but also in the great ruling powers of his life, the will, the dominant loves, the ends and aims, the motives and the delights of the whole life.— Self, centered not in the pride of a glorious intellect but in the debasement of the sensuous nature, was elevated to the throne of empire and the sanctuary of worship, and the Lord the Creator and Father was cast down. Loving themselves more than God, craving the homage and service and abject submission of their fellows to their own irresponsible rule, they cast out Charity and Mercy and Purity, and finally slew the Heir Himself, (Cain killing Abel, Gen. iv. 8.) and seized upon His inheritance. Then came the waters of the great flood and swept them all from the face of the earth. Thus was accomplished the first minor cycle of time, the first consummation of an age, the completion and end of the first church among men.

The First Silver Age.

1. We have arrived at the first great opening or gap on the circle (2348 B. C.). At this point the great Spiritual Word, the open intercourse with the heavens and the luminous perception of truth, becomes submerged in the waters of the flood (See Chart, Fig. 1, where the Word is sinking into dark waters). The internal faculties of the soul are closed up. Direct communication with the inner world ceases. The great door is shut to humanity and henceforward they must grope blindly or walk by the dim light of an external faith. Here Science, now in its feeblest infancy, takes the inner position (See the crossing of the blue line to the inner position, and the red line to the outer, at the upper part of Figure 2), and men are henceforth to be enlightened only by its faint beams, and instructed through an external method. Men, shut out from the glories of the inner heavens, now turn to the supersti-

tious contemplation of the star-lit dome of night. Possessing some traditionary doctrines preserved from the grand revealments of the past, some faint glimmerings of a far-off morning land still lingered in the night of the sad ages, and a dim symbolism of the forgotten glories came down in the twinklings of the still suggestive stars that made night mysterious. Astronomy, a faint reflex of the broad knowledges of the former age, now began its germinal existence as a purely external science. Coming more immediately into contact with external nature, and experiencing new wants from the withdrawal of the Divine protective sphere, men's necessities impelled them to a more intimate acquaintance with the surrounding objects. Thus several of the sciences date their birth back to this remote age. Something was known of metals and their uses, of woven fabrics and the dyeing of their textures, of Chemistry as connected with the preparation of the dyes, etc., of architecture,—rude though it must have been,—in the building of their habitations, of sculpture in giving expression to their rude conceptions,—innate in the most embruted natures,—of a mysterious, invisible, overruling destiny, and also of a very early production of some form of letters as the visible and audible external signs of the ideas within. When the gates of the spiritual realm were closed the doors of external nature were thrown open to the wandering steps of man. Thus was commenced the toilsome exploration of the wilderness—the long, weary and painful search for natural truth.

2. Man's supreme selfishness soon asserted itself in predatory assaults upon his fellows; and in the persistent effort to appropriate to himself everything which his superior power or skill or cunning or treachery could obtain. Might was the standard of right and brute force and physical courage were counted the highest virtues. Hence came warlike weapons and defences, walled cities and engines of destruction, and prisons and dungeons and scaffolds, the block and the stake and engines

of torture, and the arena of savage beasts, and the gladiatorial combat. Now also from the superstitious and perverted religious sentiments arose the temple and the altars of idolatry, and the horrid and cruel rites of their worship. They embodied their brutal, evil and cruel passions and lusts in their dreaded demons, and sought to win the favor and avert the wrath of those invisible powers by scenes of blood and cruelty and torture consonant with their own base passions.

3. Each of the areas is designed to represent a religious dispensation or some peculiar adaptation of truth to the condition of the race. The second (Fig. 2) represents the second great church commencing immediately after the flood, 2348 (Gen. vii, viii, ix) and extending to the call of Abraham, 1921, (Gen. xii, 1-3) at which point the *literal history* of the Scripture narrative commences. From this time forth the historicals of the Word deal with real, not allegorical personages and events.

The First Brazen Age.

1. The Israelitish Church proper commences with the departure of Jacob to Padan-aram, 1760, (Fig. 3, Gen. xxviii, 1–5) although it was not reduced to a regular system as a representative church until after the departure from Egypt. The preparation for this event was commenced in the flight of Moses from Egypt after slaying the Egyptian, 1531, (Ex. ii, 12, etc.) and was consummated in 1491 (Exodus xiv), when, we may say, a nation was born in a day.— This event corresponds in chronology with the discovery of America by Columbus, A. D. 1492, by which a new world was opened up for the birthplace of human liberty and the emancipation of religion from the bonds of the civil and ecclesiastical power.

2. From this time the history of the people representing the spiritual church to come is the record of a continuous succession of apostacies, enslavements and oppressions, repentances and deliverances—the nation at times rising to great magnificence and power,

and again sinking to the deepest humiliation and distress. Its power became greatly reduced, and ten of the twelve tribes were separated from that of Judah, the possessor of the legitimate Kingdom, and were at length carried into captivity and finally entirely lost to history.

The First and Second Iron and Clay Ages.

1. The Kingdom remained with Judah with various fortunes, suffering long periods of captivity, being often overrun and laid waste, and gradually declining from its meridian splendor under Solomon; until it became the dependency of various nations and, finally, was subject to the Roman Empire, and the nationality was ultimately lost before the time of the Lord's advent. (Fig. 4.) At this time the wickedness of the world, and especially of the Jewish nation, had become so great that demons actually had bodily control of many. This church finally consummated its wickedness by the rejection and crucifixion of the Lord.

2. At this point, A. D. 1, is the limit and extreme distance of departure. Now the day-star of the world has arisen, a new orb has burst upon the spiritual vision of the universe (Fig. 5). From this time the progress of the race has been upward on the return toward the former state. Like the decline, it is slow and gradual, making but little progress in many centuries. Indeed, after the first age of the Christian church its advance seems scarcely perceptible up to the time of the Reformation.

The Second Brazen Age.

1. About the year 1530 (Fig. 6), a new impetus seemed given to the development of the true religious spirit; the faiths were reconstructed, and the truth separated from many falsities that had been diligently sown by the unslumbering enemy of the Church. This was a renewing of the dormant spirit of the first Christian church, which, like the Israelitish church, covers two distinct ages. Thus was inaugurated an accelerated move-

ment, but one which gradually died away until, about the middle of the eighteenth century, a new descent of power was felt under the Wesleys and others.

2. From and after the reformation the tendency to division and the multiplication of sects was very strong. This was the legitimate outgrowth of the spirit of the age.— Faith, or a preëminent regard for doctrine, was the animating spirit of the movement, and every master intellect contended stoutly for his own especial view of truth. This disposition to give prominence to dogma over charity or the good of life, and its work of reducing the reformed church to a multitude of fragments, continued with little abatement till about 1857, since which time there has been a marked change, and the tendency of most religious denominations is strongly toward union.

The Second Silver Age.

1. About the year 1757 (Fig, 7), a new revelation of spiritual truth was given. This

event marks the consummation of the first Christian church and the beginning of a second. This is the return of spiritual truth to the earth, the admission of the Church from the outer to the inner courts of the Temple, the opening of the door, the lifting of the vail, the emancipation of religion from the slavery of external rites and materialistic dogmas, the unvailing of the living statue of Divine Truth as seen in the spiritual sense of the Word.

2. Not only has religion been vivified and her faith purified, but science has felt a new impulse; the vernal life of the descending heavens has caused the rapid upspringing of blade and stem and leaf; the icy torpor of earth's long winter is relaxed, aad all nature gives prophecy of returning spring. This is caused by a new descent of life into the church and into the world, a return of charity toward the earth, a going forth of the dove from the ark seeking a resting place among the desolations of the great flood.

3. Science, as it ever has done, greatly

outruns religion on its emergence into light. On this returning scale are marked certain prominent events exerting great influence on the condition of man. Among these are the art of printing, 1450, the discovery of America, 1492, the discovery of terrestrial magnetism, 1600, the invention of the Telescope, 1608, the microscope, 1665, the construction of the Steam Engine 1767, Steam navigation 1807, and the Electric Telegraph, 1844.

The Second Golden Age.

1. In nearly all events, inventions and discoveries there can only be an approximation to definite dates. Scarcely any discovery or invention or great moral or social or political revolution is made at once. The law of progress is slow and gradual, and the preparations for great discoveries, inventions or revolutions are prolonged and extended usually in the ratio of their importance.

Most of the great catastrophes in human nature that have revolutionized the whole social, civil, political and religious condition of a people, or a nation, or an age, have been simply the culmination of a long succession of preparatory events, extending over years, perhaps centuries, of time. The destruction of Jerusalem and the dispersion of the Jewish nation was the final catastrophe of a long declension in national righteousness which attained its consummation in the rejection and crucifixion of Christ.

2. So also in all great forward and upward movements of the race there had been long states of previous preparation, a gradual education of the people up to the necessary point at which combinations and organizations could take place. The operation of this law is plainly traced in the return of man to the yet-prophetical Millennial age. That time will come as surely as the earth stands; for it will be the natural consequence of a long chain of progressive movements in Religion and Science, tending continually upward, and it is but the orderly sequence of an irresistible law of the Divine government.— The very fact of the incarnation of the Lord

as a new and conquering power, and the establishing of a new order of religion and science, is a sure prophecy of the final complete regeneration of the earth in all its kingdoms and the return of the golden Age, not in its old condition of infantile innocence, but in a new innocence of wisdom and angelic manhood.

3. We may, by observing the coincidences of the great events, in the decline and the return in human history, especially in religion, which is its soul and life, arrive at an approximately correct date of the Millennial advent, in its more marked beginnings. By a reference to the Chart, it will be seen that in the first half of the circle—the retrogression of the race—there are four great pivotal dates, marking the points in the history of the human family, on which are hinged certain great eras pregnant with its destiny. The first, the beginning of the circle or the meridian of the golden age, B. C. 4004; the second, that of the flood, 2348; the third, the commencement of the

Israelitish Church, 1760; and the fourth, in the flight of Moses from Egypt preparatory to the exodus of the Israelites from captivity, 1531. Now, corresponding to these numbers on the opposite side of the Chart we have, first the Reformation, A. D. 1530 (a difference of 1 year between the Exodus and the Protestant Reformation); second, the new revelation of spiritual truth, 1757 (a difference of 3 years between the Israelitish Church and the New Dispensation); and, yet to be established, the commencement of the Millennium, 2339—464 years from 1875—(a difference of 9 years between the Flood and the Millennium), corresponding with the end of the Golden age—the Flood. Following the same system of calculation and the same ratio of increase, we find that man will complete the first grand circle on the dial of time, or meridian of the millennium, about A. D. 3977—2102 years *from 1875*—(a difference of 27 years between the two sides). It will be seen that the dates do not absolutely and precisely agree, the return time being accelerated in a certain obtainable ratio, owing, doubtless, to the increased influx of power into the world. Taking the dates as we find them, they stand thus:

Golden Age.....4004—3977=27, dif. bt'n the two sides.
Flood (Sub.)....$\frac{2348-2339 = 9,}{1656-1638=18}$ " " Flood and Mil-[lennium.

Flood..........2348 2339
Isrl'sh Ch. (sub.)$\frac{1760-1757 = 3,}{588 - 582 = 6}$ " " Is. Ch. & N. Dis.

Israelitish Ch. 1760 1757
Exodus (sub.) $\frac{1531-1530 = 1}{229 - 227 = 2}$ " " Ex. & Prot. Ref.

Another curious coincident is in the ratio difference between each product of the three examples: *i. e.*, 18, 6, 2, making $\frac{9}{18}=\frac{1}{2}$ on first example; $\frac{3}{6}=\frac{1}{2}$ on second example; and $\frac{1}{2}$ on the third example.

4. It is supposable that the commencement of the golden age was very remote, centuries if not ages beyond the utmost chronological records in our possession, and that the event marked as our second great date was at its close after a long declension. So the corresponding point marked as the probable date of the millennium, 2339, or 464 years from

1875, is at the full commencement of that period, and it may be thousands of years before its glories will be fully revealed and its blessings fully enjoyed in the complete regeneration of the human race and the purification and restoration of the natural world. We have demonstrated, in the beginning of this article that there is a spiritual science of mathematics, and that the retracing steps of a return must necessarily cover the original ground of the departure. The journey from a moral point of departure and the journey back to it, are exactly equal in length. The time occupied in each may be variant, according to impetus and the power exerted in each case. But we think there will be found little discrepancy in either half of the history.

Why Chart printed in Colors.

1. The colors on the chart are representative of the religious and scientific condition of the race in its several stages of progress. White light is composed of three primary or

elementary colors, Red, Yellow, and Blue. These are the original and uncombined colors. By their various combinations every variety and tint known to man may be and are really produced.* The red ray is the one accompanied by heat, and hence repre-

---

* An interesting proof of this may be seen by intently looking for a few moments at a bright spot of any of the three colors on a dark ground and then turning the eye to a white wall or other object, when the image of the colored spot will appear in the complementary color, not either of the three colors separately, but the remaining two combined. For instance, suppose the color selected be bright red, the image on looking on a white ground will be green—a combination of yellow and blue. The reason is obvious: by the strong action of the red light upon the retina of the eye, its susceptibility to the red in the white of the wall is for the moment destroyed,—just as bright sunshine makes us blind to objects in a dim light,—while its susceptibility to the remaining two colors remains unimpaired. They are therefore seen alone at that point while the red is excluded, and their combination together produces green. This is the meaning and the origin of complementary colors.

A very good way to perform this experiment is to paste a small piece of bright colored paper on a dark ground of any kind, and, after looking at it for a few moments, cover it suddenly with a sheet of white paper without moving the eye.

sents love, religion, charity, mercy. The yellow ray is the most luminous, and hence corresponds to wisdom, faith, intelligence.— The blue ray is the one accompanied by chemical action and is called actinic, and hence represents science, or knowledge productive. Following this order, the red line running with various windings and undulations through the circle represents religion, the blue one accompanying it with its angles and lines represents science. When religious or scientific activity is very small these streams are comparatively straight and smooth, but when the activity is greater the undulations and angles are more frequent. When these two great principles are in their purity, the tint is lighter, but where they become perverted and obscure the tint is darker and more murky. All Nature is mathematically colored. The leaves of trees are green and they correspond, in both the yellow and blue colors that compose them, to faith and Science. In the fruits, red and its combinations largely predominate. In the fruit of the vine, red and blue are the prevailing colors. In most of the small fruits red prevails, sometimes with an admixture of yellow, sometimes of blue. Of all flowers the rose is queen, and the prevailing color is red and its various shades from deep to almost white. It is emphatically the flower of love in purity. The lily, pale, faintly tinged with red, is the emblem of passionless purity.

These instances are proof of the law of color as exhibited in the chart.

SCIENCE AND RELIGION.

Corroborative Testimony

TAKEN FROM ONE OF ROBERT SEARS' WORKS.

"It is most unfortunate that science and religion should ever have been made to assume a hostile front. This has been productive of incalculable mischief, which has operated in two different directions. In the first place, it has too frequently led the friends and advocates of religion to display an unwarrantable jealousy of the progress of science, and to frown upon those who were engaged in the ardent prosecution of it. It would appear as if the imagination had been indulged, that every new conquest achieved by science, involved the loss of a domain to religion—that every new pillar erected in the temple of science had been stolen from the temple of religion. This sort of groundless alarm might have suited the time when ignorance was esteemed the mother of devotion;

and when undoubtedly it was the interest of the priesthood of a corrupt superstition that men should know as little and think as little as possible. But surely all such jealousy is unworthy of those who have an equally well-grounded conviction that the works of nature and the volume of revelation proceeded from the same source.

"If this be the case, then, while science and religion may each have their appropriate domain within which their *dicta* are absolute, it can never happen that these will be contradictory. God has not written one language in the Bible, and a contradictory language on the face of creation. Revelation and science may not always speak the same truths, but they will never speak opposite truths. The danger lies in a kind of twilight understanding of either. It is not only possible, but likely, that an imperfect knowledge of the Scriptures, on the one hand, and an imperfet knowledge of science on the other, may land us in irreconcilable difficulties, which can only be cleared away by a more complete understanding of both. But this, so far from leading us to be jealous of the advances of science, should lead us to encourage and stimulate them to the utmost. While it is not only justifiable, but right, that we should regard with suspicion any conclusion of science which seems subversive of the truths of the Bible, it would be at once irrational and sinful to attempt to stop its progress.

"Perhaps the conclusion may be a wrong one, deduced from a superficial acquaintance with science, which, if farther prosecuted, would lead to its abandonment. Perhaps the contrariety between science and revelation is only apparent, and results from our hasty and erroneous interpretation of the Bible. Take, for example, the well-known case of Galileo. He became convinced as he prosecuted the study of astronomy, that it was not the sun which revolved round the earth, as was universally believed at that time, but that the earth revolved round the sun. Alarm was taken at this conclusion, as if it expressly contradicted the language of the Bible, which speaks of the sun as rising and going down, and Galileo was subjected to persecution as an infidel. What then was the result? The science of Galileo has been established beyond the power of contradiction; but the Bible has not therefore been found to speak the language of falsehood. His discovery has only led to a sounder interpretation of those texts which the science of astronomy was thought to contradict. And this must be the issue of all seeming contradictions between revelation and science. It may happen that science now, as in the days of Galileo, may subvert some of our views of Scripture language; but, if so, we ought rather to rejoice that science has aided us to a sounder and more correct interpretation of the Bible than we had hitherto attained.

"Here, then, are two errors to be guarded against, which we shall take time merely to notice. The first is the tendency to bend the facts of science to meet our views of revelation. No attempt could be more mischievous than this. When we are engaged in examining the properties and relations of matter, let us receive the facts it gives us without equivocation and without reserve—let us listen to the voice we evoke, as if there was not another in the universe. When we set ourselves to study nature, let us become the faithful and humble interpreters of nature. The second error is, the tendency hastily to adapt the language of Scripture to the inferences of science. This tendency is no less mischievous than the other, and has led in some instances to an utter subversion of all religious truth. When we are engaged in the study of the Bible, let us deal by it as we would by science itself. Let us hear what it says without reserve, and listen to its voice as the voice of God. Our part is to act as its fatihful and humble interpreters, and to subject it only to such questionary processes as we would adopt with any other record, the real meaning of which we were anxious to ascertain. By acting thus honestly both with science and religion, it will be found that they speak a language always harmonious, because always true."

THE TWIN RIVERS;*
OR
SCIENCE AND RELIGION.
By J. T. C.

Down the continent of time,
Flow two rivers side by side; †
One with silver flood and azure,
One with gold and crimson tide.

Winding through a devious valley,
Plunging down the mountain's steep,
Down the gorge of murky ages,
Then through marshy plains they creep;

Flashing in the light of morning,
Dark and silent as the grave,
Clear as crystal now their waters,
Turbid now as Lethean wave.

---

* Written on seeing Prof. Emery's Chronological Chart, "Religion and Science."

† See Paths of Religion and Science on Chart. Religion is represented by the winding *red* path; and Science by the zig-zag *blue* path.

Winding, gliding, flowing ever,
These two rivers side by side;—
Science one and one religion,
Truth and goodness, Man and Woman,
Youth and maiden—Bridegroom, Bride!

When perverted—false and evil
Are the bitter floods that flow;
Hideous consorts! syren, demon—
Death and darkness, wail and woe!

See! the glare of conflagration
Blood-red o'er the darkness break;
Glow the fiery arms of Moloch,
Gleam the fagots and the stake.

Rack and wheel and red arena
Soaked and steaming hot with gore;
Hear the shriek of mangled victim
Rising from the Stygian shore.

Tigers snuff the reeking carnage,
Eyeballs red with rage aglare,
While the shout of maddened thousands
Rend the demon-haunted air.

Through the bleak and gloomy ages
Crimsoned o'er with human blood
Slowly wind the turbid rivers,
Slowly pours th' empurpled flood,

Sinking deep and slowly deeper
In the death-o'ershadowed vale;—
Till the hour of earth's deep midnight
Woe and darkness shall prevail.

O'er the darkness of the ages
With a phosphorescent light,
Pale as moonbeams through the vapors
In the ghostly hours of night,

With a flickering, flashing lumen,
With a dim, unsteady gleam,
Science o'er the darkened ages
Sends her faint, uncertain beam.

Lo! a gleam of star or planet
Streaming 'thwart the midnight sky,
Rising o'er yon eastern mountain,
Resting now on Calvary!*

Pale, pure beams of pearly brightness!
Silver sheen of holy light,
Streaming through the silent darkness,
Silvering all the robes of night—

Pale, prophetic star! thy glory
Breaking now o'er mountain height
Tinges all the coming ages
With a warm millennial light!

---

* See Cross at bottom of dial on Chart "Science and Religion."

Clearer flows the purple river,
Purer burns th' uncertain ray,
Growing brighter as the darkness
Slowly lightens into day.

Purple now to crimson paling,
Crimson pales to flamy gold;
Murky azure fades to silver
As the pearly gates unfold.

And these twinn'd and winding rivers,
Sparkling in the morning ray
Soon shall swell into an ocean
In the full millennial day.*

On yon mountain midway rising
To the stooping, bending skies,
See the million millions gathered,
Hear the songs of triumph rise

Like some grand celestial Organ;—
"Earth is ransomed; sin and tears,
Death and hell have passed forever,
Never more to be remembered
Through the long, eternal years."

---

* See the Word as it emerges from the cloud at upper right hand of Chart "Religion and Science."

APPENDIX.

A BRIEF BIOGRAPHICAL SKETCH

OF

THE AUTHOR

BY

W. F. WOODWORTH, M. D.

ALSO

A

Written Delineation

of his

PHRENOLOGICAL CHARACTER

BY

PROF. O. S. FOWLER.

Why This Appendix.

The Divine Teacher said, "He that doeth evil hateth the light; but he that doeth truth cometh to the light, that his deeds may be made manifest." So confident are we of the truth of our works, now offered to the public, that we come forward with Portrait, Biographical Sketch and Phrenological Character, that they may see and know us the more intimately. We recognize their right, in some sort, to know him whom they are asked to read; and perhaps in no other way can they so readily gain the desired insight into his character as by a view of his face, his life, and his mental and moral characteristics. Besides, a short biography is often very useful as showing the triumphs of courageous and determined effort in overcoming great difficulties and in winning the battle over great opposition.

The Author.

Biographical Sketch.

By W. F. Woodworth, M. D.

---o---

Every great work creates a desire to see and know something of its author; hence Prof. Emery, who deprecates anything like self-laudation, has so far yielded to the wishes of his friends as to insert here the briefest* possible sketch of forty-four years of his life.

He was born Sept. 12th, 1830, in Franklin Co., Ohio, of German descent. His father—Rev. S. J. Emery—was an eminent clergyman. His mother, fourteen years an invalid, was a sterling Christian woman.

---

*He expects at some future time to publish a more full biographical sketch, in which will be related some wonderful things which are too numerous and lengthy for this brief sketch.

At three years of age, scarlet fever came near depriving him of life, and left him a semi-mute. He has never recovered his hearing, nor entirely his health.

As a youth he was remarkable for many useful and curious inventions, evincing great originality of thought, and an insatiable thirst for knowledge which, for want of hearing and means, was beyond his reach.

At eighteen, his mother, for whom he had a peculiar affection, died, which intensified his naturally spiritual cast of mind, already strengthened by his social seclusion and years of filial companionship at the maternal sickbed.

At twenty-one, to use his own phrase, he was "profoundly ignorant;" but I opine that to a mind like his, the physical world, to him so mute and mysterious and yet so beautiful, furnished many "object lessons," fraught with the choicest self-culture, and suggestive of the measureless height and fathomless depth of the Infinite ; and that in taking counsel of his heart at the bed-side of his invalid mother, in so many years of filial duty, he acquired much of that mental discipline and self-abnegation, which distinguishes his later years. If, then, he was "profoundly ignorant," he had the best possible foundation upon which to build a fine character and embellish it with choice culture and rich attainments; otherwise his subsequent almost magical development would seem a miracle. He now entered the Indiana Deaf-Mute Institution, and in *one year* passed through its seven years' course, and for nine years thereafter was one of its successful teachers.

Seven of these years (after he was twenty-two years old) were devoted faithfully, earnestly and untiringly to severe study; mostly of the natural sciences—some thirty branches in all,—among them Astronomy, Chemistry, Geology, Botany, Radiology (radiates), Entomology (insects), Ichthyology (fishes), Herpetology (reptiles), Ornithology (birds), Ethnology (races of men), Physiology, Anatomy, Phrenology, Physics (matter, heat, light, etc,), Political and Domestic Economy,

Natural History, Architecture, Landscape Gardening, Mental and Moral Science, etc. etc.

To accomplish so much, he made it a rule to retire regularly at 9 P. M. and to rise at 3 A. M., excepting Sundays.— This rule he strictly adhered to the year round. During most of the seven years he boarded and roomed at the Indiana Deaf and Dumb Institution. This building being heated by hot air from a furnace in the basement, and the fires never lighted till about 5 A. M., his room would not become warm till near 6 o'clock; and the furnace often getting out of order, there would be no fire for a day or two. Of course, in winter it was very cold work to study for hours and often days without fire, and sometimes the cold was so intense that it was impossible to stand it. After dressing, washing etc. (which he *always* attends to, and does yet on rising), he would on those cold occasions take the bed clothes and spread on a chair, seat himself and pull them snugly over him, and thus tucked up would go on with his studies uninterruptedly. Thus he succeeded in keeping up his studies regularly through the winters.

This plan gave him ten hours' study per day, five hours in the morning and five in the evening, besides his hours of teaching. This, including his Sunday studies of Moral Philosophy, the Scriptures, etc., made an average of 75 hours per week; making for the seven years, 27,300 hours of hard study besides his regular duties as teacher which he faithfully performed.

All this was accomplished without the stimulus of great aspirations for honor or personal aggrandisement, but from a desire to learn for himself all in his power of every branch of truth; with the full hope that the wiser he became the happier and more useful he could be in his isolated condition, and the wider would be his influence and the greater his opportunities to benefit his fellow creatures, and especially those of his peculiar condition. And he has not been disappointed in these hopes and these desired opportunities ; for he says he often feels well paid for all this toil by the satisfaction it has afforded him to witness the evident gratification and benefit many have derived (learned men as well as others) from listening to and conversing with him about the Arcanas of nature and Spirit—and especially of the latter. For it is through a clear understanding of the one that he can more fully and clearly read the other.

This habit of study he still maintains, though he does not rise so early now as then.

During this time, by this severe private study he acquired literary and scientific attainments which won him the degree of M. A. from an Indiana College.; being, I think, the first semi-mute in America receiving that distinction.

At twenty-six he married Miss Mary Alley, of Decatur Co., Ind., an accomplished deaf-mute lady, and a graduate of his Alma Mater.

In 1860, desiring a wider and freer field, he went to Kansas, passed through the famine of that year, refusing public relief, and during the war which followed, by great personal exertion and sacrifice, he succeeded in establishing the Kansas Deaf-Mute Institutute, and published a literary paper, called the Kansas *Home Circle*. Subsequently he published the *Marseilles* (Ill.) *Independent*.

His Kansas enterprises were not remunerative, and he came out of them with impaired health and depleted purse ; and turning his mind more exclusively to the application of science to theological research, found in the high way of science, the open way, "through nature up to nature's God," in the "science of correspondences."

For seven years, amidst trials and discouragements, but with sublime faith in his mission, he devoted the best energies of his mind to his chart, "Order of Creation," illustrating his theory of creation, and showing the harmony of spiritual essence with physical substance.

By the aid of this chart he demonstrates that all creation is based upon the exact science of mathematics, thus founding the universe upon the one immovable rock of truth, and showing the orderly relation of the natural sciences from Chemistry to Ethnology—the progressions of creation from the lowest or gaseous to man—called by modern scientists the "Descent of man." This he shows to be by an orderly *ascent* from lower forms as bases or continents, to higher ones superimposed upon them, as a structure upon its foundation, which he proves to be the normal method of creation instead of the development of lower into higher orders as denoted by the doctrine or hypothesis of evolution.

For the last three years he has also, by great study in the direction of the mathematics of history, designed and perfected his Chart, representing the conjoined pathway or history of Science and Religion, illustrating the fall or declension of man from order and innocence and wisdom, and his redemption through a new influx of truth into the natural and spiritual degrees of the soul. It also shows a curious mathematical method of figuring out the incoming of the Millennium, by tracing the coincidence of certain great events both before and after the coming of Christ.

These Charts, with his books, are really very remarkable productions, especially so for a self-educated man, and he a semi-mute, almost isolated from the world and cut off from its numerous advantages; shut up, so to speak, within himself, and thrown entirely on his own resources. They transcend anything known in the "silent world," and the charts are certainly unequaled by anything of the kind ever attempted by any one.

As an educator he takes high and advanced ground; always radical and progressive, he stands high among his contemporaries.

He accepts no theories, however well supported by learned opinions and venerable traditions, until he has examined their structure, handled their pillars, and digged about their foundations to see whether their substratum be rock or sand.

I cannot do better in this connection, than to quote from a writer in a Western journal concerning the subject of this biographical sketch:

"Prof. Emery is glorified in one of our editor's letters, as well he may be; for few men have ever contributed to the relief of suffering humanity so bountifully—none certainly with greater readiness or with warmer sympathy. The *Home Circle*, though a prodigy of perseverance and industry, is not an accidental development of his energies. He has been singularly sagacious and original in devising ways and good ones.

"Our friend, casually observed, has nothing particularly striking in his personal appearance. His present defects are timidity and a distrust of his own abilities. By plying him with questions, the whole mental make-up of the unpretending man will be brought out in striking contrast to the entire awkwardness of the 'outer man.' One would pass him in the street half a dozen times without notice; but once drawn into a disquisition with him on scientific subjects, such a one would find his conversation a sort of

German punch, made up of philosophy, education, medicine, architecture, and religion. He has a natural, felicitous flow of talk, always overswelling its boundaries, and sweeping everything before it right and left. He is very earnest, intense, emphatic.

"Perhaps our readers may imagine that our remarks relative to the Professor have all a leaning to favoritism. We take leave to quote the opinion of Mr. E. A. Sheldon, Superintendent of the celebrated 'object' school at Oswego, N. Y., with regard to his views of education:

"'I am glad that Kansas is represented by one, at least, who has correct views of education. It is quite gratifying to find one who is so thoroughly Pestalozzi*; and to you it must be equally gratifying to find that your views so nearly accord with those of one whose name stands in the front ranks of the educational reformers of the *world*.'

"Mr. J. A. Jacobs, A. M., for many years superintendent of the Kentucky Institute for

---

* Referring to the founder of the system of object-teaching, Pestalozzi.

deaf-mutes, in a letter dated the 14th of August, 1862, pronounced the Professor's views of education to be 'entirely just.'

"We then are not alone in the opinion we, on our own side, have already expressed on the subject.

"His dress is usually plain, but scrupulously neat.

"He has 'it in' him to achieve the proudest triumphs* and the greatest laurels, considering his phrenological developments."

Personally, Prof. Emery is plain, retiring and unpretentious, caring little for outward show, valuing only internal adornments.

His great depth of thought, ripe scholarship, spiritual premonition and sterling qualities of mind and heart are best appreciated by those who sit down with him to " the feast of reason and flow of soul."

---

* When this was penned Professor Emery was Superintendent of the " Kansas Deaf Mute Institute," of which he was the founder, and little dreamed at that time that this prediction would be literally fulfilled in the production of his Charts and books, especially his work on " Order of Creation," which was first thought of of some time after leaving Kansas.

Notwithstanding some defects in pronunciation, resulting from defective hearing, his fine mental acquirements, good language, earnestness and sincerity of manner make him a very interesting public speaker.*

Socially, he is warm and true-hearted, genial and sincere.

Morally, no guile has been seen in him, in a long and intimate acquaintance.

The future, with its measureless possibilities, is before him. That his usefulness may be commensurate with his exalted aims, is the earnest hope of his life-long friend.

---

* Acquired mostly since he was 35 years old.

PHRENOLOGICAL CHARACTER.

Phrenological Sketch.*

Given at Indianapolis, Ind., Jan. 27, 1857.

By Prof. O. S. Fowler.

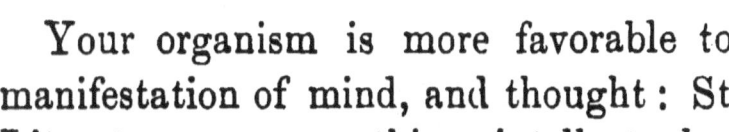

Your organism is more favorable to the manifestation of mind, and thought: Strong Literature, or something intellectual, than of anything physical, such as labor of any kind. You are active physically and quite strong, in fact, for a man of your health, very strong and also spry, and tough, and could endure labor if obliged to, but your

---

* His father, who was a fine Physiognomist by nature, self-study and experience only (never having read any works on Phrenology and Physiology) pronounced this Phrenological description very accurate in details.— Though in doubt as to all the claims of Phrenology, this was to him a practical proof that there was something, if not a good deal, in it.   Ed.

organism runs naturally much more to the mental than material, and sentimental than Physical, and I perceive that your forehead is hot, which signifies an unusual action, especially of the intellectual organs. You have within five years been studying with all your might, or reading, writing, and thinking.*

Have had a great many ideas, and they have been based on common sense; you have become dissatisfied with many doctrines taught you, and have *investigated for yourself*, and have exercised a more than ordinary share of sound, available common sense.— Have very likely studied nights, which I charge you not to do, and sleep abundantly and not exercise your mind too many hours in the 24, but exercise your muscles more,

---

* This was given 5 years and 4 months from the time he commenced his education, beginning with the "Manual Alphabet" 3 days after he was 21 years of age, and is part of the time mentioned in Biography where it speaks of his private studies. See page 97 of this work. Query, How did Prof. F—— know this, they being entire strangers; or by what sign, &c. did he read this knowledge so accurately?   Ed.

and mind your eating, for though your stomach is naturally good, it is now practically poor, I presume in consequence of overeating, a disease of some kind.

I somewhat think that you have been the victim of *Quinine*,* and I charge you to take no medicines, but instead take care of your health. Give yourself abdominal action by swinging your hands, Gymnastics, or some kind of manual labor, for your *vital* and digestive organs are becoming torpid and your brain unduly excited. Breathe deeply and be much in the open air, and especially cultivate conjugal affection, plant your attachments where they are to remain for life.†— You will find washing all over in cold water every day of great service to you. You are a *most ambitious* man, but your ambition runs mainly in the line of *intellect, and moral.*—

---

* Just previous to this he was sick, and the Doctor gave him quinine; he has taken none since. What sign shows the effect of quinine? ED.

† He had been married just 6 months and 2 days. Is there no sign by which to know married persons from unmarried ones? ED.

You are ambitious to keep your moral character *pure and spotless*. You are ambitious to excel in whatever you engage. You are determined to use the world to the best advantage. You are wanting in self-respect, too distrustful of your own abilities, too excessively alive to the speeches of people.— You are rigidly just to govern by correct motives. Very hopeful, buoyant, and aspiring, and look naturally on the *bright side*. No way *revengeful*, but very resistant, forcible, and calculated to push your plans, right through, thick and thin. You are hearty in your friendship, but rather particular, so that if persons are not exactly to your liking discard them, and this principle will appertain in regard to your choice of a wife.

So make up your mind to marry at least soon, and secondly to cultivate conjugal affections, and let nothing interfere with it. In two years* after marriage, for once fairly enlisted, your attachments will be hearty.— You are fond of children, friends, and home,

---

* Does man only become "fairly enlisted" some time after, instead of at marriage?

and will enjoy domestic life very much if suitably matched.

You are likely to dwell on one single thing till it is all done up, and are very continuous.* You are no ways *revengeful*, yet are quick-tempered, but *govern* your temper well. You are liable to eat too much and too fast. I spoke before Physiologically, now Phrenologically when I repeat, eat less and leisurely. You are very fond of money —will make everything pay. You have a good mercantile talent—are close, but *honest*. You are exceedingly cautious and reserve, even down to minor matters.

You should cultivate outspoken frankness. You are too fearful of consequences by all means. Shake off much of your anxiety, for it does no good, but rather does you harm. You have a good deal of religious sentiment, especially of spiritual premonition. You are devout and very obliging, but hard to believe unless you have proof which cannot be

---

* Hence his success on Charts, "Order of Creation," 'Circular Chronology," &c.   Ed.

gainsayed nor resisted. You are kind and full of sympathy, but do not give money as freely as kind offices. Possess rather a brilliant Imagination along with excellent descriptive powers, and if properly educated could make a first-rate writer. You are exceedingly fond of the beautiful in Nature, and art, the poetical, the perfect, and are particularly fond of the flowers, of Literature and elegance everywhere. You have really refined taste everywhere, and in everything. You have, too, Mechanical ingenuity,* but *ought not* to live by manual labor. You are too serious,—ought to laugh more and joke. You are a great observer, see every thing, and remember all you see. You are great in method, want everything in place. You are good in figures. You have the

---

* His first mechanical effort was a nice case-knife handle made when nine years old. At ten he invented a correct sun-dial that read the hour, half and quarter hours from sun rise till sun set, he never having seen or heard of such an instrument. Got the idea by seeing his mother make a "*noon-mark*" on the porch. At 23 made, with a jack-knife, a sextant that read the minutes,—never having seen one. Since then, he has invented a great number of things.   Ed.

Phrenological organs requisite for making a good minister.* You remember places well, and have an almost unconquerable desire to see as well as try the experiments. Have a historical cast of mind; you are logical and excellent in putting this and that together —very discerning. See minor points of difference and discrepancies. You have of late been studying some subject deeply.† Will command an excellent style of expression.— Language is well developed and words well chosen. You are agreeable, have a well-balanced mind, but, sir, I repeat, your health should receive your first attention, for it has suffered badly.

Relief is by a rigid observance of the Laws of health.

---

* He was early impressed that he was called of God for special work, and thinks he is serving God in all he does; and also thinks that he was specially endowed and directed to work out the "Order of Creation," Circular Chronology, &c.

† Architecture, which he then thought of following as a profession at some future time. How can a Phrenologist tell this? Ed.

A Masterly Production!

Arcana of Nature Revealed!!

ORDER OF CREATION,

OR

The Orderly Creation of Man.

BY P. A. EMERY, M. A.

A beautiful, illustrated chart, showing the order of creation, based upon Mathematics and constructed upon strictly scientific principles. Showing the relation and natural position of various kingdoms and the orderly arrangement of the natural sciences: and illustrating the orderly *ascent* of creation, from its first inception to its crown of perfection in MAN:

WITH A

MANUAL OF EXPLANATION:

To which is added The Twelve Axioms of Creation and amplifications of the same.

Address MRS. PROF. P. A. EMERY,

Chicago, Ills.

☞ This profound and wonderful chart is so original and unique it must be seen to be understood and appreciated.

A Wonderful Book.

Inner Life Night Thoughts,

OR

The Rational Dream Book.

ILLUSTRATED.

By P. A. Emery, M. A.

A treatise based on new laws of interpretation, rational, scientific and logical: it deals in no conjectures or fanciful interpretations of dreams, but philosophically and scientifically explains their origin, their significance, and their *use*. A book designed to show how to read character by dreams, and for the improvement of same in all.

"Dreamland is a play-ground of the soul,
Weird regions vast, like unto death profound.
* * * * * * *
May see and know—and, being seen,
Tell others what a dream may mean."

Address Mrs. Prof. P. A. EMERY,

Chicago, Ills.

☞ This wonderful book comes next to the Bible in teaching us what we are, and unvails self-deception. It should be in the hands of every one—saint and sinner, old and young.

www.ingramcontent.com/pod-product-compliance
Lightning Source LLC
Chambersburg PA
CBHW020117170426
43199CB00009B/555